FAMOUS RAILWAY PHOTOGRAPHERS

H. C. CASSERLEY

Skye bogie No 14279 quietly coming 'on shed' after its spell of duty — 17 June 1927 — taken from a hill on the outskirts of the city of Inverness, overlooking the Moray Firth.

My first visit to Scotland and about my first sight of the Highland Railway.

FAMOUS RAILWAY PHOTOGRAPHERS

H. C. CASSERLEY

DAVID & CHARLES
NEWTON ABBOT

0 7153 5631 3

Printed in Great Britain
by Latimer Trend & Co Ltd Whitstable
for David & Charles (Publishers) Limited
South Devon House Newton Abbot Devon

INTRODUCTION

A good many years ago, – just about a quarter of a century in fact, and a not inconsiderable span of one's normal lifetime, I was one of a few selected authors, I think about a dozen in all, of a series of small paper backed booklets published just after the war under the title of 'My Best Railway Photographs'. A very modest and somewhat immature effort, indeed, but in fact one of my very first books.

I now feel fortunate and privileged to be invited to participate in a somewhat more ambitious series on the same lines, and to be grateful that I have survived to be still 'in the running' as it were to take my place among my numerous younger successors in this particular field. How many of my old time contemporaries have also attained this distinction I cannot at the time of writing say, but I do hope that two or three of them, at any rate, will be around to enjoy this distinction.

To go back to the beginning, however, now, over half a century ago, when to be meticulously specific, I made my very first exposure on 14 December 1919 at the old New Cross sheds of the *LB&SCR* in company with the late J.N. Maskelyne, then an experienced railway photographer himself, who very kindly came along to give me a few useful wrinkles. I started under some of the worst conditions that can be encountered, on a dull winter's day and my first picture, of a Brighton D tank No 264, although it 'came out' more or less satisfactory, was not of sufficiently good quality to be able to reproduce here in a book, the negative having deteriorated over the years so as to make it impracticable to produce a satisfactory print suitable for blockmaking. Only a fortnight later I was able to attain a real scoop in the shape of the first ever published photograph of the new Midland 0-10-0 on its first trials; this is illustrated on page 11 together with more details of the event. Although this occurred right at the beginning of my railway photographer's career I have never again had such an epoch making discovery, as in later years advance publicity usually became the order of the day (although there was of course Gresley's 'hush-hush' engine of 1929, No 10000). Official and commercial press coverage also became more widespread, apart from the growing number of amateur railway photographers — a somewhat rare species in my early days.

A brief description of the equipment I have used over the space of half a century, which comprises only three different types of camera, is given on page 94.

When one is using photography as a means to an end, that is, as in this case, obtaining a permanent record of the changing railway scene, it is wise to get thoroughly used to a piece of equipment and stick to it without experimentation. One just cannot run the risk of failure after travelling long distances to obtain particular subjects, the opportunity for which will probably never again arise. The same applies to materials used, as much to-day as ever; find out what brand or type of film you get on best with, and keep to it with foreknowledge of what treatment it needs to obtain the best results.

Fifty years ago even the fastest emulsion speeds were rated no more than 500 H & D, by the system then in vogue, whilst the Panchromatic film or plate was still in its infancy. This I soon found very desirable for railway photography in bringing out the reds and yellows more truly, particularly the latter, as with ordinary non-Panchromatic material, yellow lettering and numbers, especially on buffer beams, tended to be entirely invisible.

I found also that glass plates gave very much superior results to roll films (and that invention of the devil, film packs), the great disadvantage being of course bulk and weight, and severe limitation of numbers available without a dark room change. Even with a maximum of about thirty slides — no inconsiderable load to cart around — one had to be extremely careful and selective in what one took on a day's outing. There could be no indiscriminate firing-off with thirty-six exposure 35mm film with plenty of reloads in the bag, as in these days, and it sometimes happened that a maddeningly attractive subject would crop up near the end of the day when one had used all available material.

The problem of plate changing was of course most difficult when on holiday, and it became necessary to do the changes under whatever variable conditions one might find in a hotel bedroom. I usually found a wardrobe the best answer, sitting outside and working within with the door open, but even then one could be bedevilled by ill fitting or inadequate window curtains, with a street light outside, or even a glass fanlight over the door. As a last resort operations had to be carried out under the bedclothes, uncomfortable at the best of times, hot and sticky, and dealing with recalcitrant plates which got stuck in the slide, conditions which on occasion would have provoked even Saint Peter to blasphemy! Not making any pretence of such high standards it is not difficult to imagine the blueness of the atmosphere on these occasions! When I visited the north of Scotland in June 1928, this was however the only answer, as it is quite light even at midnight in these latitudes. On this particular occasion, I think it was at Wick, it seemed unusually hot and uncomfortable, and I discovered that there was a hot water bottle in the bed, which one hardly expects in midsummer! There was also another infernal device known as a changing-bag, in which one worked inside a light-proof bag with one's arms through a couple of vents fitted with elastic bands. I never got on with this, for one thing with your hands imprisoned there was no means of scratching one's ears or nose, which seemed always to require urgent attention at these times.

This particular Scottish holiday is also memorable for the amount of material I had to carry. I had a large suitcase three quarters full of boxes of plates, gradually being transferred from 'unexposed' to 'exposed', and naturally carefully labelled to prevent tragedy – hardly any room for such impedimenta as spare shirts, socks, and However, I managed somehow or other to hump all around Scotland in ten days and to bring it safely home.

I was still using plates on my first three or four trips to Ireland, and remember a few agonising moments on one occasion while going through customs at Dun Laoghaire or Holyhead (I forget which), when one officer was suspicious of the contents of my boxes of plates and wanted to open them to see what was inside! This would of course have spelled disaster to my precious exposures. I think I had to appeal to a higher authority, who fortunately took an understanding view of the matter.

As to subjects covered, these of course can include a wide range of variety and interest. Somewhat naturally my first efforts were of solo locomotives. I suppose most of us started this way, or at any rate with conventional moving train shots, but in later years my interests widened considerably, particularly in respect of such things as stations and general railway scenes, coaching stock and so on, much neglected in the earlier years.

Until Leica days, however, restriction of the number of photographs it was possible to take in a single day's outing without change of plates inevitably restricted the choice mainly to locomotives, of which there was such a superabundance of invaluable subjects. It was simply not possible to allow for such things as coaching stock, later to become a most interesting sideline, and one can only regret that the 35mm with its much wider range of possibilities, did not exist in the 1920s, when so much valuable material had to be ignored in consequence. Even before the eventual complete demise of steam increasing standardisation was beginning to narrow the interest in locomotives themselves, and more attention was being paid to subjects of more general interest, stations in particular. I had always been very interested in railway history and geography in general, apart from actual locomotives and trains, and by the beginning of World War II had succeeded in travelling over a very large proportion of the railway system of Great Britain and Ireland, although not quite to the extent of the late renowned T.R. Perkins, who had a much earlier start in the days when closures were virtually unknown. With my son's increasing interest in the same thing, however, I had almost to start all over again in the 1950s for his benefit, and so came to cover much ground for a second time, and also some new fields previously unexplored. Later of course he was able to get around on his own, and to a large extent catch up with me, although there were by that time many cases where this was no longer possible.

Although I have never practised to any extent the kind of super-arty pictorial photograph so much in vogue in more recent years, where the engine and train itself are of secondary importance to the setting, surroundings and atmosphere, I have at the same time always tried to inject as much pictorialism as possible into even the most humdrum photograph, often very difficult at such locations as running sheds, although even there one was sometimes able to choose viewpoints with a pleasant background of trees, or something of that sort. I tried to avoid too many conventional side of three-quarter solo loco views, filling the whole picture space and showing nothing else; some sort of background was generally quite practicable. Rear views of locomotives are frowned on by many, but sometimes this was the only possible viewpoint, and better than nothing at all. Some classes of locomotive seemed moreover to photograph better from some angles than others, sometimes even from the rear end. Remarkable how they often differed in this respect, but I suppose the same might be said about human beings!

In early days I went after very little but the oldest engines, which were not likely to last long, modern ones I more or less left alone, not looking far enough ahead and feeling that they would always be there. In this way I missed out on a good many subjects which I ought to have taken in the early 1920s, and in particular on new styles of painting as in the first years of the grouping, many of them short lived and of considerable scarcity. I was careful not to make the same mistake when nationalisation came along, and again at the beginning of the diesel age, much as I disliked the diesels, I did not try to pretend that they were not there, and got a fairly representative collection of some of the unsuccessful earlier types which have already disappeared.

Foreign railways never attracted me, and apart from two brief pre-war excursions just across the Channel I have never been abroad. I felt it preferable to specialise in covering as much as possible of the railway systems of Great Britain and Ireland, which offered quite as much as I could cope with in my limited time available, and I have never regretted this.

Nowadays one has to go overseas in search of main line steam, and apart from age consideration I would not wish to go in at the 'tail end' as it were, following already well-worn trails on the heels of so many others, and only finding the remnants of better days when I got there.

Colour photography I have never gone in for apart from a few isolated experiments, but I did in fact take what I think must be one of the earliest railway scenes on colour film, a *SE&CR* 0-6-4T from the end of my garden at Bromley in 1936. Even at that time, however, with pregrouping days not such a distant memory, I felt that colour photography had come too late to be of much interest for railway purposes, notwithstanding that engines were kept clean in those days. This is not to belittle the very fine colour photographs that have been taken in recent years, particularly during the end of steam period, but one nevertheless regrets that such materials and techniques could not have been invented a decade earlier, when colour really meant something, so far as a locomotive and train are concerned. There are also few things more difficult to photograph satisfactorily than a grimy engine.

I do very little outside work nowadays; there is so little left to make it worthwhile going chasing around here and there, apart from considerations of age. I still obtain much pleasure in reprinting old negatives and coming across many which have never been printed of subjects long forgotten, taken during the intensive earlier years since the war when I was taking far more photographs than I could possibly print at the time. I find that retirement now gives me the time to catch up to some extent, and I still continue to do all my own processing.

I can only conclude by being very thankful that I was born just about the right time to have remembered the railways in their heyday, from pregrouping days through to nationalisation, and more regrettably to their general decline. With no longer any incentive, even if I had the ability, to get around very much, I can now pass my declining years in peace and tranquility, living largely on memories.

I make no apology for this illustration, although it has appeared several times before, the first in fact within a very short time of its being taken at Derby on the 1 January 1920, when it appeared in the old 'Locomotive News'. The first illustration to be published anywhere, and I believe actually the first picture ever taken of the new engine in steam, official or otherwise.

Many rumours had circulated from the closely guarded precincts of the works, almost as inaccessible at that time to outsiders and to the press as the Kremlin, as to the nature of this engine, which was known to be under construction, but the details of which remained a closely guarded secret until it first saw the light of day.

Anyway, there she stood, to my utter astonishment, on that sunny New Year's Day of 1920, opposite the north end of No 6 platform, perfectly situated for a photograph, even if a little too far away, and fortunately being unobserved – things were somewhat strict at that time, especially on a secretive line like the Midland, I was able to obtain what was a reasonably good shot, considering that I was at that time only just beginning the art of photography.

Although I think it was the first picture of it ever taken in steam, Mr J.B. Radford's recent book does show a hitherto unknown official picture of it taken in the works before it had been steamed, on 27 November, 1919.

It was then only the second ten coupled engine ever to work in this country, the first of course having been the short-lived *GER* Decapod of 1902.

This was a particularly difficult photograph, and one which I have always been rather proud of, having been taken under the most unfavourable conditions of a fog of 150 yards visibility on a dull day, 3 February 1934.

No 311 was at that time the last survivor of Mr Johnson's original 4-4-0s built in 1876/7, thirty engines in all, none of which was ever rebuilt with larger boilers as were all of their numerous successors. It spent its last days on an easy job, quietly meandering over the plains of the *LNWR* line between Peterborough and Northampton. On this particular day, knowing of its imminent withdrawal, I went out on the 9.25 am from St Pancras, then taking the branch train to Higham Ferrars, oddly enough with a *S&DJR* 0-4-4T No 1230, walking thence to Irthlingboro' in time for the 2.41 into Northampton Castle station, which I had good reason to believe No 311 would be working, as indeed it was, to my great satisfaction.

The original of the Johnson single wheelers, regarded by many, including the author, as the most handsome engines ever built, was in its last years used for working the directors' saloon from Derby, from which centre it was liable to travel all over the system, and which it continued to do for a few years even after the grouping until its withdrawal in 1928. It was the only one of its class to receive slight modification in the shape of a Deeley cab, as seen in this illustration, taken at Derby on 29 July 1922.

It was one of the few which survived to recieve *LMS* painting, still of course in Midland lake; none of this class ever suffered the indignity of the desecration of *LMS* black.

The London Tilbury & Southend Railway, absorbed by the Midland Railway in 1912, must naturally fall into the category of that company's all embracing system. It was mainly a holiday and residential line, but it also served the important port of Tilbury. Throughout its existence the passenger traffic was worked by 4-4-2Ts of three main varieties, of which No 2175, featured here, was one of the 'intermediate' class, built as No 68 *Mark Lane* in 1903. With two exceptions all *LT&SR* engines had names in Tilbury days, but these were rather regrettably removed when taken over by the Midland.

This view of Upminster, taken on 22 August 1926, was before the District line extension over the site of the tracks to be seen on the right hand side of the picture.

The Somerset & Dorset Joint Railway was jointly owned by the old Midland and the *LSWR*, the former being responsible for the locomotive stock and operation of the line and the latter for the civil engineering.

The engines, although independently maintained at their works at Highbridge, and with their strikingly individual blue livery, were largely of Midland design and origin, many of them being built at Derby, as was No 46, featured here, being in fact the last new passenger engine for the Somerset & Dorset, turned out in 1928, before the locomotive stock was absorbed into the *LMS* in 1930.

It was actually one of a batch of seventy, then under construction for the *LMS*, one of the Midland types adopted as standard for new construction, and was to have been No 580. Being urgently required by the *S&DJR*, it was however appropriated, together with two others, which became Nos 44 and 45.

When the Somerset & Dorset was taken over in 1930, the three *S&D* engines became *LMS* Nos 633-635. Photographed at Derby when new on 22 July 1928.

DIGNITY AND IMPUDENCE. Facing up to each other at Derby on 16 June 1928 are a veteran of 1869 and a newly constructed 'Royal Scot' No 6141 *Caledonian.*

No 1200 was the first of a class of twenty-six engines built by Matthew Kirtley in 1869/70, most of which spent almost their entire long lives on suburban work in the London area, and in their last years on empty stock work and general shunting duties. Until demise of the last few in the early 1930s, there was rarely a time when two or three of them were not to be found in and around St Pancras. After their final and very much regretted departure the grand old station never seemed quite the same, and as one who remembers them so well I can still even in this diesel age, feel that their ghosts still haunt their old domain.

Like the *S&DJR*, the Midland & Great Northern Joint also had its own locomotive stock with works at Melton Constable, and again its distinctive yellow livery, very much like Stroudley's 'improved engine green' although in later years changed to a shade of medium brown.

The majority of the engines were again of Midland type. Most numerous were the small 4-4-0s of Mr S.W. Johnson's design of 1876, but introduced to the *M&GN* in 1894. Some were later rebuilt with larger boilers, as were most of their *MR* counterparts, but the majority remained in their original condition, apart from the provision of extended smokeboxes.

Until taken over by the *LNER* in 1937 these engines worked practically all the main line duties on the *M&GN*, often with prodigious loads, considering their small size, on the heavy holiday traffic on Saturdays during the summer season.

No 3 is seen here making a vigorous start out of South Lynn on 24 June 1929.

For many years the *M&GN* had struggled on with elderly engines maintaining its main line services; indeed it never had any new ones of any sort after 1909, but in 1936 the position was slightly alleviated by the loan of two Johnson class 3 4-4-0s Nos 758 and 759 from the *LMSR*, which were put on the most important trains of the day, the through workings between Nottingham and Yarmouth. *M&GN* drivers, faithful as they were to their old charges, admitted that these were the best engines they ever had. No 758 is seen here pausing at South Lynn on 1 July 1936, with the through train from Yarmouth to the Midlands.

After the *LNER* took over the working of the line in 1937 such types as *GER* 4-6-0s and 4-4-0s were drafted to the line, and in later years *LMS* type Ivatt class 4 2-6-0s took over most of the working until closure.

Even the briefest coverage of the Midland would hardly be adequate without including one of the famous Deeley three cylinder compounds, of which forty-five had been built by the *MR* itself (five of these being reconstructions of the original Johnson design of 1901). After the grouping it was adopted by the *LMSR* as a standard express passenger class, no less than 195 additional examples being turned out between 1924 and 1932, a further order being cancelled by Mr Stanier on his arrival from Swindon, as he had entirely different ideas on the subject, the full story of which has been recounted several times elsewhere.

With moderate loads within their capacity these engines could take their place amongst the most efficient ever seen in this country. Naturally they could hardly be expected to undertake the heaviest express trains which would fall to a large 4-6-0 or a pacific, although they came very near to this on the Caledonian and *G&SWR* sections, where they probably did their finest work.

No 41064, one of the first of the post grouping ones, seen here leaving Derby with an up express on 11 June 1949, already renumbered but still in *LMS* livery.

My first introduction to the Highland was rather curiously at Inverness itself. Most travellers would have had their initiation at Perth, or possibly Keith or Elgin, if travelling by the east coast route via Aberdeen. In my own case, however, I was making my first visit to Scotland on a more-or-less conventional tour with a non-railway friend, and we travelled up the Caledonian Canal from Fort William by the old paddle steamer *Gondolier,* a slow but lovely journey taking all day, no longer possible and much too leisurely for the present generation of car and motor coach travellers. Naturally on arrival at Inverness in the late evening I was itching to see my first Highland engine. I went along to the station where the only one around was the station pilot, 4-4-0T No 15011, standing in smart *LMS* livery; hardly surprisingly it fired me at once with an enthusiasm which had got to be vigorously followed up.

This first short stay at Inverness was somewhat cramped by the necessity of falling in with my friend's general interests, although I did manage to visit the shed and obtain a fair sample of the good things to be found.

It was obvious however that I would have to go up again on my own and devote my whole and undivided attention to the railway. This I did in the following year when during a hectic ten days I managed to cover the whole of the line and branches, see all of the engines (four of which were away at St Rollox works and had to be run to earth there on my way back) and photographed many of them.

This picture, taken on 19 May 1928 on Britain's most remote branch, with 4-4-0T No 15013, was of course the ultimate goal in this connection.

I remember that on presenting my through tourist ticket at St Pancras, made out to Lybster, the outward half of which I managed to retain and still have in my collection, the collector remarked 'You've a long way to go!' – remarkably he knew where it was!

Prior to the introduction of more modern engines, express working over the Highland was almost entirely in the hands of the nineteen 4-6-0 'Castles' built between 1900 and 1917, and eight 'Clans' which came out in 1918. The 'Castle' in particular was a very fine design, with coupled wheels of only 5ft 9in to cope with the mountainous grades, they nevertheless had a good turn of speed on the level and downhill stretches, and had proved so reliable that when new engines were urgently needed in 1917 three more were built, as in the case of the 'Lochs' mentioned on page 20.

No 14693 *Foulis Castle* was the last of these, and is seen here piloting an earlier example, actually the first of the class, No 14675 *Taymouth Castle* on the overnight 'Royal Highlander' from London, leaving Perth about 6.00am on 22 May 1928, both stalwarts preparing to do battle up the gruelling ascent to Druimuachdar, including the formidable last eighteen miles from Blair Atholl, almost entirely unbroken climbing and much of it at a one in seventy gradient.

One of the most useful classes the Highland possessed were the Lochs, of which fifteen were built by Dübs & Co in 1896. Three more appeared in 1917 to the same design to meet urgent wartime requirements for additional engine power; it was deemed preferable to perpetuate a well established reliable class rather than a more modern, but untried, design.

No 14393, *Loch Laochal*, is seen here on 15 May 1928 at Dalnaspidal, highest main line station in the British Isles, after having piloted a southbound train up the long ascent from Aviemore.

My objective on this occasion was the 1484ft summit at Druimuachdar, two miles to the north of the station, and as I was walking along the adjacent road the driver stopped the engine, then running light back to Aviemore, and very kindly gave me a lift to the summit.

Having reached the highest point on any standard gauge main line in the country, I had almost three hours before it would be necessary to return to Dalnaspidal to continue my journey to Inverness. I had hoped for rather more activity than there was during this sojourn; I was in fact able to photograph only two freight trains during the long wait. The first was northbound in charge of one of the famous Jones goods, No 17924, one of the fifteen engines built in 1894 and well known as being the first 4-6-0s in Great Britain.

I was fortunate with a gleam of sunshine when this train appeared, on what was a mainly cloudy, but luckily dry day.

After what seemed an interminable time, during which my only refreshment available was a drink of pure Scottish mountain water 'out of the burn', at last a southbound freight appeared. Not in charge of a Highland engine, but what was for me at any rate the next best thing, a Fowler class 4 0-6-0 No 4314, of Midland design, but of course *LMS* built. Seven of these engines, Nos 4312-4319, then being turned out in large numbers, for use all over the *LMS* system, had been allocated to the Highland, and spent a good many years up there before being drafted south.

Quite likely the only picture of a Midland and Highland engine taken together, although there is the possibility of Jones goods No 103 in its restored condition having met up with an *MR* engine in its travels at somewhere like Kingmoor. Kirtley 2-4-0 No 4 was however almost certainly the only genuine Midland engine ever to penetrate so far north. Other Midland designs – *LMS* built – such as class 4 goods, did indeed make their appearance (see page 22).

Why it was ever sent is something of a mystery; it was said for trials on the Kyle of Lochalsh line, but this seems improbable, as it would not have been particularly suitable for the numerous curves. Anyway it was photographed here at Inverness on 21 May 1948, together with *HR* 'Strath' class No 14271 *Sir George*. Its No 4 contrasted strongly with all the five figure numbers which surrounded it.

Although one could not but admire the greatly improved appearance of Highland engines in their smart *LMS* red livery (as at first applied to all passenger engines) I was glad to find a few still retaining the rather dull Highland green. Amongst them was one of the three small 0-6-0Ts built by Stroudley during his short stay at Inverness before assuming control at Brighton, where of course he produced his famous 'Terriers', of which the Highland engines were antecedents.

No 57B Lochgorm, photographed at Inverness on 21 May 1928, five years after the grouping, and where it had been built in 1872, over half a century earlier. It survived to become *LMS* 16119, and was not scrapped until 1932, after a life of sixty years.

The Highland had the double attraction of not only possessing one of the most interesting collections of engines to be found in the country, but also of being one of Britain's most spectacular scenic routes, with such contrasts as the lush valley of the rivers Tummel and Garry, through Pitlochry and the Pass of Killiecrankie, the wild stretches over the Grampian mountains, the bleak moorlands of the far north through Sutherland and Caithness to Wick and Thurso, and the magnificent Kyle of Lochalsh line with the lovely last few miles along the shores of Loch Carron.

These two views taken respectively on the 29 and 20 July 1931, depict two of these contrasts, the first one being of a north bound express, including Pullman car, crossing the bridge near the 'Soldier's Leap' on the River Garry, before plunging into the short tunnel, from above which the picture was taken, thence through Killiecrankie station and Blair Atholl, after which the scenery changes to the wild moorlands on the long ascent to Druimuachdar summit, 1484ft above sea level (see pages 22 and 23).

The second scene depicts a southbound express, this time with a Midland clerestory dining car, near the second highest summit, Slochd Mhuic, between Perth and Inverness, 1315ft above sea level.

In both these views the engine is one of a series of ten Horwich 2-6-0s, Nos 13100-13109 (eventually BR 42800-42809) built in 1928 and allocated to the Highland railway, the first importations of a new *LMS* type for express working. They spent a few years on these duties before being replaced by the ubiquitous Stanier Black Fives, which worked much of the main line traffic until the diesel age.

By coincidence the 2-6-0 in both views happens to be the same engine, No 13105, in the case of the Killiecrankie view acting as pilot to one of the 4-6-0s built in 1915/6 for the Highland, but found to be too heavy for some of the bridges and taken over by the Caledonian as Nos 938-943 on that line, later *LMS* 14756-14761, of which this one is 14757.

After the grouping the bridges were strengthened and it was found possible to transfer the engines to the Highland, for which they had been originally intended.

It was in 1925 that I first turned my attention to light railways, starting with the famous Stephens group, which being mainly in the southern counties, were the more accessible for me, living in South London as I did at the time. First of all was the Kent & East Sussex; I still have vivid memories of my initial trip over the line, and although I was unfortunate enough to have to travel in one of the extremely uncomfortable Ford petrol railcars for part of the journey, it in no way diminished the fascination of such a primitive backwater, with its miscellaneous selection of elderly engines, and whetted my appetite for further similar adventures.

This view was actually taken on a later visit, on 14 March 1931, when with the lady who later became my wife I combined the railway aspect with a visit to Bodiam Castle and other local features more to her interest (poor girl, she did not realise what she was taking on!).

The train from Robertsbridge is seen here with former *LSWR* Beattie 0-6-0 No 9 *Juno*.

Another of the railways controlled by Lieut Colonel Stephens – himself something of a railway enthusiast who managed to combine pleasure with business – was the Chichester & Selsey, or Hundred of Manhood & Selsey Tramway, to give it its correct title. It was also later known as the West Sussex Railway. Opened in 1897, it led a precarious existence until omnibus competition forced its closure in January 1935.

This view at Chichester station (which was situated in a yard adjacent to the Southern premises) on 5 November 1928, shows 2-4-2T No 1 Selsey, the only engine built new for the railway, others being saddle tanks of varying vintage, mostly Manning Wardles, obtained second hand at different times from sundry sources.

The Shropshire & Montgomeryshire was a line of early origin with the unique distinction of having been twice closed and abandoned and subsequently resuscitated. The first period, when it was the Potteries, Shrewsbury & North Wales Railway, lasted from 1866 until 1880. It was reconstructed by a new concern, the Shropshire Railway, in 1891, but never actually reopened, and again fell into decay. However, along came Colonel Stephens in 1907, who formed a new company under its later title, constructed under the Light Railways Act, and reopened it in 1911. It was ultimately requisitioned by the War Department in World War II, a large number of ammunition dumps being built along its route, being finally closed in 1960.

Amongst the collection of old engines which I found on my first visit on 28 August 1926, the most ancient of all was this 0-4-2ST No 2 *Severn*, originally a 0-4-0 built by Bury as long ago as 1840. Already derelict, although not actually broken up until 1932.

The Bishops Castle Railway, another unfortunate line with a chequered career, but which managed to maintain a precarious existence from its opening in 1866 until its final demise in 1935. Amongst the several engines it owned at various times the best known was *Carlisle,* which worked most of the traffic in later years. It was originally built by Kitson & Co in 1867, being reconstructed to its later form on acquisition by the Bishops Castle in 1895.

It made a very pleasing sight standing in the bay platform at Craven Arms on 30 May 1932, when I paid my one and only visit to the line. Painted in bright green and kept in well-polished state, it will be noted that it had acquired something of a Great Western appearance, with its chimney and other details, which it acquired in later years when it was sent to Wolverhampton works for major overhaul.

The Easingwold Railway, 2½ miles long, had the distinction of being the shortest standard gauge railway in the country.

Opened in 1891, it ran a passenger service until November 1948, and was finally closed in 1957. Throughout its life it only possessed two engines, and then only one at a time.

No 2, illustrated here, was built by Hudswell Clarke in 1903. When it was under repair, and after being scrapped about 1948, an engine was hired from the *LNER*.

On the occasion of my visit, depicted here on 30 June 1933, I had just taken this picture when an excited elderly gentleman appeared, violently brandishing an umbrella, and demanded to know what right I had to be taking photographs on private property without permission. Not knowing the exact answer to this one, as it was undoubtedly a privately owned railway of which he claimed to be the owner, I had to talk gently, but I managed to mollify him to the extent of his agreeing to my taking further pictures, not to be published. A condition which I of course duly observed, but which could hardly apply after this lapse of time.

The 2ft 0in gauge Ashover Light Railway was opened as recently as 1925, one of the last railways new, standard or narrow gauge, to be built in this country. It was intended to serve the pleasant country town of Ashover, Derbyshire, by connecting with the Midland main line at Clay Cross. Unfortunately it came at a time when road transport was already an established alternative method of transport for such a service and comparatively short distance (7½ miles) and its life was short, passenger traffic being discontinued in September 1936 and closed altogether in 1950.

The six engines, of which *Joan* is one, seen here at Ashover on 23 October 1926, were all of USA design, built for use in World War I in 1917.

The Campbeltown & Machrihanish always presented something of a challenge, a railway which must be done somehow. Perhaps because it was Scotland's only independent light narrow gauge railway, but possibly even more because it was the most inaccessible line in the British Isles, and needed a whole day to make a visit possible. An important consideration with so much to do in such a limited amount of time.

Anyhow, I managed to work it in on 2 August 1930, several hours from Fairlie Pier, reached from Glasgow Central behind *G&SWR* 4-4-0 No 14376, and back in the evening from Wemyss Bay with *CR* 4-6-2T 15350 – great days!

It was a rough voyage and the boat was about an hour late at Campbeltown, leaving me with the difficult decision as to whether to visit the shed, some distance away, where I knew they had two other engines, or 'do' the line to Machrihanish – there was no time for both. Fortunately I made the right one, to travel over the line, the opportunity could never present itself again as it was closed two years later.

The train on the quayside at Campbeltown, with Andrew Barclay 0-6-2T *Atlantic* awaiting departure.

The Wantage Tramway, one of the last roadside lines of its kind, operated between Wantage Road, on the *GWR* Bristol main line, and the pleasant Berkshire country town of Wantage. Passenger service ceased in 1925, but freight continued for another twenty years, and this view was taken on May 10 1930, showing such a train in charge of a veteran 0-4-0WT No 5, with an interesting history. Built by George England & Co of Hatcham Ironworks for the Sandy & Potton Railway, it later came into the hands of the *LNWR* and is believed to have worked on the Cromford & High Peak Railway for a time. It was sold in 1878 to the Wantage Tramway, on which it worked for the rest of the line's existance. Restored at Swindon in 1948 it stood on a plinth at Wantage Road until that station was closed, and is at present housed by the *GWR* Society at its Didcot premises.

Before the 1923 amalgamation the Isle of Wight possessed no less than three independent railways, of which the Isle of Wight Central was the largest, although the Isle of Wight was rather better known to holidaymakers, serving as it did the three important centres of Sandown, Shanklin and Ventnor. The third railway was the Freshwater, Yarmouth & Newport, with only two engines.

All of these became part of the Southern system at the amalgamation.

IWCR No 4, seen here at Sandown on 11 June 1923, was one of a pair of diminutive 2-4-0Ts built by Beyer Peacock in 1876. It became W4 in the Southern list and was scapped in July 1925.

The Isle of Wight Railway was worked almost entirely by a series of 2-4-0Ts, again by Beyer Peacock, seven of them in all, built between 1864 and 1883.

Wroxall at Shanklin on 1 June 1921 with a Ventnor-Ryde train. Painted in a red livery, they were not numbered in *IWR* days, but this engine became *SR* W16 at the grouping and lasted until July 1933.

An interesting and now largely forgotten fact was the contrast between the whistles of the two railways' engines, which could be seen together at Ryde and Sandown. The *IWR* was extremely shrill, somewhat like the Great North of Scotland, whereas the *IWCR* had Caledonian type hooters, later adopted on the *LMS*.

The Whittingham Mental Hospital in Lancashire was a large institution served by a short length of railway from Grimsargh, on the Preston-Longridge branch, for the conveyance of coal and other supplies, and also visitors (carried free of charge).

At the time of my visit, on 21 April 1951, there were the two engines shown here, No 2, built by Andrew Barclay in 1904, and a Stroudley D tank No 1 *James Fryars,* obtained from the *SR* in 1947, originally *LBSC* 357 *Riddlesdown.*

In organising this visit, attended by about twenty members, the thought occurred that the authorities might regard us, some of whom had travelled some two hundred miles for the sole purpose of traversing a short one and a quarter miles length of railway, as suitable candidates for admission to what was in those days still referred to candidly as a lunatic asylum, or in more popular jargon, a nut house. Anyway, we managed to get away safely without being detained for examination.

The Edge Hill Light Railway, opened in 1919 to serve the ironstone deposits of North Oxfordshire and Warwickshire, was another line with which Colonel Stephens was associated, of which he was appointed engineer. Its 'main line', which connected with the Stratford on Avon & Midland Joint Railway at Burton Dassett, was worked by two of Stroudley's well known 'Terriers', Nos 1 and 2, late *LBSC* 673 and 674 (originally *Deptford* and *Shadwell*). Its period of operation was short, the quarries ceased production in 1925 and the engines were left derelict in the open – they never had a shed – where they stood without turning a wheel for over twenty years, subject to the ravages of time and the elements (vandalism as we now know it had not yet reared its ugly head) until they were eventually cut up on the spot in 1946.

This view shows No 2 standing forlornly on 8 June 1939. It will be noted that the old *LB&SCR* initials are beginning to show through the later coat of paint.

The first of the very many photographs I ultimately took in Ireland was this one obtained in the early morning at Waterford on 14 September 1929 on my arrival from Rosslare.

Jumbo was one of a small number of *G&SWR* locos regarded as departmental engines and which were unnumbered. It had originally been built at Inchicore in 1876 as a 0-6-4WT and was reconstructed as a 0-6-0T No 202 in 1895, spending its last working years shunting at Waterford, being in fact not broken up until 1957.

I discovered early that Irishmen loved being photographed and seemed to think that I had come over there especially for this purpose. On this occasion I had to take the photograph in a hurry as there were others appearing on the scene from all parts, and a minute or two later there would have been hardly any engine visible. One had to do the best one could on these occasions.

The main objective of this first day in Ireland was the Waterford & Tramore, which had an old 2-2-2WT No 1, built by Fairburn in 1855, still in regular use, although it was not working on this occasion. I was able to get it pulled out of the shed for photographs, but I had to await a subsequent visit before I was able to see in action and ride behind it. This view, taken on 7 July 1934, by which time it had become *GSR* No 483, shows it entering Waterford terminus on its 7¼ mile journey (without intermediate stations) from Waterford.

This line was entirely isolated from the main system on the other side of the river Suir.

The engine might have had an even longer life had it not derailed itself in 1935, falling down an embankment, from which recovery would have been difficult, and it was unfortunately cut up on the spot. Together with the Caledonian single (p89) withdrawn about the same time it had been the last single wheeler in regular use in the British Isles, although there were a couple of North Eastern 2-2-4Ts still hauling inspection saloons until 1936-7.

My first visit to Ireland in 1929 was concerned almost entirely with the railways of the Free State, chiefly embracing the Great Southern, both broad and narrow gauge.

It was not until the following year that I was able to turn my attention to the north, and as a Midland lover I was very naturally completely captivated by the *LMS* owned Northern Counties Committee, formerly the Belfast and Northern Counties, which had been aquired by the old *MR* as long ago as 1903. By 1930 it was in effect a miniature edition of the Midland, from the red livery applied to all engines and carriage stock, to the engines themselves, largely of Derby design and some of them actually built there.

Amongst the many delights I found on this system was this charming little 2-4-0 shunting at Londonderry, one of several built by Sharp Stewart and Beyer Peacock in the 1870s.

A pity that colour photography was then unknown, as this black and white can hardly do justice to the lovely vision, spick and span in crimson lake with polished brass beading to the splashers.

Taken 6 August 1930.

The Great Northern *Enterprise* express from Belfast to Dublin passing Dundalk on 15 May 1950. This was one of Ireland's crack trains, and covered the 112½ miles between the two cities non stop in 2¼ hours.

No 208 *Foyle* was one of five engines built principally for the service by Beyer Peacock in 1948.

They were the last engines of the old established 4-4-0 design to be constructed in Great Britain and Ireland and possibly in the world. With the exception of the two *SL&NCR* 0-6-4Ts mentioned on page 52 they were also the last new steam engines built for any Irish railway, and all of them only too soon to be superseded by the inevitable diesels. When the Great Northern Railway Board, as it had been since 1953, was finally disbanded in 1958 and the locomotive stock divided between the Coras Iompair Eireann and the Ulster Transport Authority, No 208 was one of those apportioned to the latter, becoming *UTA* 58. As such it lasted only until 1965.

Whilst the standard gauge for Ireland main line railways is 5ft 3in, there was a considerable number, mostly built during the last years of the nineteenth century, of the narrower 3ft gauge, especially suitable for the more remote and outlying areas. This one, however, the Cork & Muskerry, was more of an urban affair, and the train seen here is running along Western Road, Cork, also used by electric trams until about this time, (10 June 1932) – note the overhead wires still in position.

The engine is a 4-4-0T, No 2, built by the Falcon Engine Co in 1887, one of half a dozen owned by the *C&MLR*, and a type which also found favour on some of the other narrow gauge lines. This railway closed in 1934.

The Fintona tram was unique in recent times as having been for many years the last horse worked passenger railway in the British Isles. This picture, taken on 21 April 1948, with my son on the upper deck, shows the branch 'train' setting out from Fintona Junction, after making connection with the Great Northern of Ireland Londonderry-Enniskillen main line, at a full five mph for Fintona terminus, about half a mile distant.

This is the only 'train' I have ever encountered from which it was possible to jump off en route, race on ahead, take a photograph, and rejoin while still in motion, as on this occasion.

This method of operation continued until the closure of the main line by the Northern Ireland Government on 1 October 1957, which was also the death knell of the still independant *SL&NCR* by depriving it of its principal outlet to the rest of the Irish railway system.

Up in the remote north west corner of Ireland, in County Donegal, was the Londonderry & Lough Swilly, together with the associated Letterkenny & Burtonport Extension, all virtually worked as one system. With a combined route length of ninety nine miles, it was the longest narrow gauge railway in the British Isles, being constructed to the 3ft gauge so widely used in Ireland. The through 74½ mile journey between Londonderry and Burtonport, its furthermost extremity on the shores of the Atlantic Ocean, occupied some four hours, through very fine wild moorland and mountain scenery. My one trip up the line, with an overnight stay at Burtonport, remains one of my very treasured memories.

The train is seen here ready to leave Burtonport on the morning of 24 July 1937, headed by No 12, one of the two 4-8-0s built for working the line, unique in being the only 3ft gauge tender engines, and the only engines of their wheel arrangement ever to run in Great Britain or Ireland.

Another remote outpost, in this case not only the farthest west railhead in the British Isles, but actually in the whole of Europe. Valencia Harbour was at the end of a long 39¼ mile and very scenic branch of the standard (5ft 3in) gauge system of the *CIE* in County Kerry.

I made this fascinating journey twice, the first time in 1934 and again in 1955 for the benefit of my son, then in process of covering as much of the Irish system as was still open, and still possible mainly behind steam. He can be seen in the middle distance, of this photograph showing the nearest railpoint to America, which would be St John's, Newfoundland, over 2000 miles across the North Atlantic.

It was necessary to spend the night in Cahirciveen on this occasion. The engine was No 127, one of the ubiquitous J15 0-6-0s of the old Great Southern & Western Railway, the only class which could in any way be regarded as standard, totalling over a hundred engines, numerous by the standards of that country.

No account of the railways of Ireland, however brief, could omit that curious oddity in the heart of the country, Limerick Junction, situated at the intersection of the Dublin-Cork main line and the secondary cross country line between Limerick and Waterford, the four principal cities and towns of Southern Ireland.

The station consists of a single platform, with bays at either end, the long face accommodating the two main line trains, which sat facing each other like 'a couple of Kilkenny cats' as E.L. Ahrons once put it. The main feature of its lay-out was that every train from whatever direction could only reach its platform by a reversal movement, although the lay-out has recently been altered so that some trains now have a straight run-in. The general pattern of the service is that trains from all four points are there at one time to provide interchange with one another. After a brief period of activity the station assumes a restful tranquility for several hours before the arrival of another batch of trains.

This scene, on 11 June 1932, shows 4-4-0 No 312 on a Cork-Dublin train and 4-6-0 No 405 with a Dublin-Cork express. The two bay platforms are out of sight in the background.

The Belfast & County Down Railway was an interesting little entity on its own before it was swallowed up into the Ulster Transport Authority, which with its anti-rail policy proceeded to close down most of the system in 1950, leaving only the busy line to Bangor, which had, and still has, one of the very few commuter business services to be found in Ireland, now of course worked by diesel railcars.

In its later steam days, its total of thirty locomotives comprised no less than twelve different classes, one 2-4-0 tender engine, four 0-6-0s of three distinct varieties, four large 4-6-4Ts, one 0-6-4T, four 2-4-2Ts (two types), one 0-4-2T, the remainder consisting of 4-4-2Ts, again of two classes, one of them comprising twelve engines, the only one which could in any way be described possibly as 'standard'.

One of these, No 30, is seen here leaving Belfast on 17 April 1948 with a typical suburban train to Bangor.

This particular engine is now preserved in Belfast Museum.

View on the Sligo, Letrim & Northern Counties Railway, near Florencecourt, on 18 April 1955. *Lough Erne,* one of the final two 0-6-4Ts, built by Beyer Peacock in 1949 (and incidentally the last new conventional steam engines for any Irish Railway) pauses with the daily through goods from Enniskillen to Sligo.

We both travelled throughout in the brake van, except for the last stage when my son was up in front on the footplate. It was here that I was unexpectedly promoted to the temporary position of goods guard, or 'tail end Charlie', as this breed was sometimes irreverantly known among railwaymen. Halting a few miles out Sligo, the orthodox guard suddenly grabbed his bicycle and got down on to the track, with the injunction 'You can take her in from here', Apparently he lived somewhere nearby, and could save himself a considerable ride. 'Quite easy; screw it down a bit passing O'Toole's farm.' Then he pedalled off down the road. I had no idea where this farm might be, and I cannot recall the actual name, but this seems as good as any, and it always seems to have such a delightful Irish flavour. I managed somehow, and we arrived safely in Sligo, but surely this could only have happened in Ireland.

A happy memory of two unforgettable rail tours, each of a week's duration, organised by the Irish Railway Record Society in conjunction with the Railway Correspondence & Travel Society and the Stephenson Locomotive Society, which took place in 1961 and 1964. They were steam hauled throughout and covering a large proportion of the railway system of Southern Ireland.

This view shows the train at Attymon Junction on 7 June 1961, in charge of the last 2-4-0 to run in the British Isles, a Midland Great Western loco built in 1897.

This engine worked us over the Loughrea branch and on discovering an old six wheeler standing in a siding we asked the stationmaster if it could be attached to the main train for the benefit of any who wanted such a unique experience at this late period. 'Sure and begorra' – fixed up immediately, on the spot. One can imagine the red tape which would have had to be cut for such a request over here – 'I'll have to refer it to headquarters' – or some sort of process which would have made even such a simple operation as this impracticable.

Another railway, an early favourite of mine.

LSWR Beattie 0-6-0 No 286A, a veteran which owed its continued existence to the incidence of World War I, when many engines were retrieved from the scrap heap, underwent yet a further shopping and repaint, and arrived back at Strawberry Hill on 1 October 1921 as seen here.

I was a frequent visitor to this shed at that time; the shedmaster (as he would have been known in later years) was very accommodating, and in company with a friend I used to go there on many Saturday afternoons, when one of the three under foremen, who worked on a three week alternating roster, was particularly obliging, and would get any engine out for photographing, if it were movable. The allocation varied from modern Uries to a fine collection of ancients, such as the one seen here, and there were usually one or two visitors from other parts of the system. The old shed still stands, in use as an electric depot.

At the other end of the system, 30 May 1922, one of three surviving Beattie 2-4-0Ts at Wadebridge. Recently rebuilt with Drummond boiler, but still retaining stove pipe chimney, wooden buffer beam, and other details, I could not then know that they were destined to survive nearly another forty years, with further renewal, and to become so well known to an entirely new generation of enthusiasts.

This was my very first trip to the West Country, and was undertaken almost, if not entirely, to seek out these already venerable engines. It so happened that the shed foreman was on holiday, and was deputised by a young apprentice from Eastleigh, whose interest seemed concentrated on the young lady at the station bookstall. Anyway, it was midday, and he took her down the road to the local hostelry, 'leaving me in charge' as he put it. The only time I have ever, even if only nominally, acted as shed foreman! Of course, nothing happened, if there had been an engine failure or derailment I knew where I could find him in an emergency.

LSWR Drummond T9 4-4-0 No 284, as superheated by Urie, descending Hewish bank with a West of England holiday relief train, August Bank holiday Saturday, 1928. These remarkable engines were employed on main line duties for many years after they had nominally been superseded by other larger types, and some even lasted until the early 1960s.

Meldon Viaduct, on the London & South Western main line between Exeter and Plymouth, now closed as a through route with the central section between Meldon Quarries and Bere Alston, bordering Dartmoor, entirely abandoned. This magnificent wrought iron structure, built in 1874, is now, since the demolition of some other equally fine ones, such as Crumlin in South Wales and Belah in Yorkshire, one of the very few still surviving, and even this has now only temporary use as a road bridge giving access between Meldon Quarries and a new reservoir under construction, due for completion in 1972.

This view, taken in 1922, shows an up Plymouth-Waterloo express headed by Drummond T9 4-4-0 No 117, then in original condition.

On my marriage in 1931 I was able to achieve a long cherished ambition of living in a house by a main line railway. The choice was not too easy, as another requirement was for a good steam service by which I could commute daily to my work in London. However I found just what I wanted on the South Eastern section of the Southern Railway, handy for Bromley South station, which enjoyed a reasonable service of non stop steam trains to Victoria and Holborn Viaduct, mainly from Gillingham and Maidstone. As the house faced north, being on the south side of the line, conditions were ideal for most of the day for photography and I secured at least a couple of thousand shots like these two from the bottom of my garden during my seven and a half years residence there.

The first view, taken on 18 April 1938, shows an up Gillingham train headed by one of Wainwright's exceedingly handsome D class 4-4-0s. Even though shorn of the elaborate *SE&CR* livery with all its embellishments, it still presented a very fine sight; as will be seen it is in spick and span condition. The shed foreman at Gillingham at that

time took a great pride in the turn out of his engines, even to the extent of removing the paint from the brass beading around the splashers, which Ashford consistently again painted over when the locos of this class, of which Gillingham had an allocation of about ten, passed through the shops.

The second view, 29 August 1931, shortly after taking up my new abode, shows a down Maidstone East line train leaving Bromley South climbing the one in ninety five gradient past my house, with rebuilt Stirling B1 class 4-4-0 No 1444.

Apart from these two examples of semi main line trains, there were also of course the Kent Coast expresses and the Continental boat trains, on all of which a variety of engines were to be seen, ranging from 'Lord Nelsons', 'King Arthurs', 'Schools', 2-6-0s, etc down to 0-6-0s and miscellaneous tank engines.

Several very happy years passed before the decision to extend the electrification to Gillingham and Maidstone drove me to seek pastures new.

To supplement the two pictures shown on the preceding pages this is just one of several hundred similar views I have chosen to depict the scene from the windows of my house.

The engine in this photograph taken on 1 June 1936 is 2-6-0 N 1890, rebuilt from the solitary 3-cylinder version of the 2-6-4T 'River' class (see page 60).

During this period I kept with the help of my long suffering but also valiantly co-operative wife when I was not there, a detailed record of all the engines seen, and which ones worked a selected range of trains from day to day, so far as it was possible to observe them. For use after dark I had a long range powerful beam torch, the large numbers on the engines in use at that time made the numbers easily readable, and I often got a toot from the enginemen who after a time got used to this somewhat unusual procedure.

Anticipating what would be 'D' day, 3 July 1939, when the steam residential service was due to be electrified, I had no intention of commuting by 'juice wagon' so long as it could be avoided, and in any case I now needed a larger house, so explored the railways north of London, then all steam worked, with a view to finding somewhere else to live, again of course with a lineside view. It eventually boiled down to the *LNWR*, at that time and for many years to come the most exciting main line out of London, even if it has now become the least interesting of all, from the point of view of variety.

After some searching, I found a plot of land adjacent to Berkhamsted station which was being developed, and was able to have a house built to my own requirements with a good outlook on the railway, the only snag being that in this case the sun was the wrong way round so far as satisfactory conditions for photography were concerned, but this did have compensating advantages. I was even able to have the siting of the house set to the exact angle I wanted it (it being at the end of a cul de sac) so that the trains could be seen from nearly everywhere in the house, excepting only one spare bedroom, the bathroom and the 'smallest room in the house'! Here I have lived ever since, apart from an enforced interruption during the war years, and hope to end my days. Steam working of the business trains on a diminishing scale, luckily lasted just up to the time of my retirement at the end of 1964.

This view shows the westerly aspect, taken in the early morning, one of the few times when conditions were right, an up Bletchley train on 14 June 1944, with Prince of Wales class 4-6-0 No 25673 *Lusitania.*

Comparing this with the picture opposite, the keen eyed observer may wonder about the similar appearance of the summer house in both views. It is in fact the same one; I dismantled it at Bromley and had it transported to my new home for re-erection. What a large variety of engines and trains it has seen in its time!

One of the ill fated 'River' tanks at Redhill on 2 October 1926. The Sevenoaks accident in 1927, when No 800 *River Cray* was derailed at high speed, resulted in their immediate withdrawal and conversion to 2-6-0 tender engines. Mention of No 800 reminds me of my earlier reference to film packs. In July 1926 I had visited Brighton and photographed – as I hoped – this engine when new out of works. Unfortunately this exposure was made on one of these unreliable devices, the principle of which was that after each shot a length of black paper drew the exposed film to the back of the pack, leaving the next on in place. On this occasion something went wrong, and all twelve hopeful exposures were taken on the same film! My picture of this unlucky engine should have been on one of these films, and I never again got the chance of taking it in its original condition.

The locomotive exchanges of 1948. One of these experiments included the dispatch of *SR* 'West Country' Pacific *Yeovil* No 34004 to Scotland for trials on the Highland lines, on which it accredited itself very satisfactorily.

It was worked north for the purpose on 2 July 1948 as pilot to Royal Scot No 6159 on the 4.55pm Belfast boat express from Euston, and I made a point of travelling on the local to Tring, which departed at the same time, in the hope of getting a carriage window shot. This worked out just right; the local had forged ahead of the express and despite calls at Watford and Boxmoor, the section between there and Berkhamsted found the two trains running neck and neck and I was able to obtain this interesting shot. Note the Grand Union Canal on the right.

LSWR Adams 4-4-0s No 0460 built by Neilson & Co in 1884, seen here at Torrington on 19 June 1926, with a train for Halwill over the newly constructed line, the North Devon & Cornwall Junction, nominally an independent concern, but worked by the Southern Railway, and to all intents and purposes an addition to the old *LSWR*. Opened on 27 July 1925 the last standard gauge rural branch line to be built in the country, it was worked for a time by these Adams 4-4-0s, the mixed train usually consisting of one passenger coach and such wagons and vans as required. Later these were replaced by rebuilt Stroudley E1R 0-6-2Ts, and finally by *LMS* type 2-6-2Ts, remaining steam worked almost to the end. Passenger services ceased in March 1965, and it is now entirely closed.

The Brighton 4-4-0s were curvaceous creatures. Apart from the running plate and cab, there is hardly a straight line to be seen. The original lot, the B2s, the first of which came out in 1895, could hardly be described as very efficient, being very much underboilered, and even in their rebuilt B2X condition, as here typified by No 319 *Leconfield* photographed at Battersea Park on 30 April 1921, they were not very much improved. All had disappeared by 1933. Their successors, the B4s, introduced in 1902, were a very much better job; some were later completely renewed with Belpaire boilers, superheaters, piston valves, and so on, but even so the whole class lasted no longer than 1951.

The practice of double heading varied greatly between the companies in pregrouping days. On some lines, such as the *MR*, *LNWR* and Highland, it was an everyday sight, whilst on others it was almost unknown. On the *LB&SCR* it was extremely rare, and this interesting shot taken at Clapham Junction on 30 April 1921 shows two 0-6-2Ts, E4 No 500 and E5 No 587, on an empty stock train to Eardley sidings. No doubt working thus for convenience sake to avoid line occupation by a light engine, certainly not of necessity from a loading point of view.

Clapham Junction was an absorbingly interesting station in those days. Then (as now) it saw more passenger trains in twenty four hours than any other in the country. But whereas nowadays at least 99% must be electric multiple units (we used to dub them 'juice wagons'), at that time more than half would be steam trains. Also whilst the locos were mainly *LSWR* and *LB&SCR*, those of almost any other railway running into London could be seen at times. I never saw a Great Central or a Metropolitan loco there, but all the others were observed either frequently or infrequently. They got there mostly off the West London line, or the North and South Western Junction, usually on freight or other miscellaneous duties. *LNWR* engines worked through regularly over the Brighton line to Norwood Junction.

One of Stroudley's well known coupled express engines, *SR* B174 (formerly named *Fratton*), seen here on 18 March 1928, leaving the old *LB&SCR* station at Epsom Town on an up semi fast train to London. An up local, with D1 0-4-2T, is standing in the siding preparatory to backing into the old station, seen in the background. After the grouping the old *LSWR* station, through which Brighton trains used to run on through centre roads without platforms, was rebuilt to accommodate both lines' services, and the *LBSC* station was closed. The small running shed can also be seen on the right.

The engine that really started it all.

I was born and spent the early years of my life near to the *LB&SCR* between Clapham Junction and Wandsworth Common, and have very clear recollections of the railway in the late Edwardian years from a footpath alongside the line when some of the engines were still in Stroudley livery. One day in 1912 however, I happened to see the new 4-6-2T No 326 *Bessborough*, then running trials and in shop grey, and thought 'what a magnificent engine', as indeed she was. It was this that first spurred me to obtain a penny notebook and to record all the engines I saw then and subsequently, never abandoned until the diesel age and even now maintained in a somewhat half hearted matter, over a period of sixty years.

Unfortunately I never had the opportunity of photographing the engine in Brighton days, whilst it still bore its name, regrettably removed by grouping, and must therefore content myself with this shot secured at Brighton on 30 April 1932.

Although I was unlucky in photographing *LB&SCR Bessborough* as such, in spite of several attempts to run it to earth, I did at least get its Great Western namesake. This was one of Dean's Badminton class 4-4-0s, built in 1898 as No 3295, later renumbered 4103.

This photograph was obtained at Salisbury on 31 May 1929, working a through Portsmouth-Cardiff train during the last years of its life as it was broken up in 1930. The Great Western at this period decided to dispense with larger wheeled four coupled engines for passenger working, and all of *Bessborough's* sisters disappeared between 1927 and 1931.

Although never a real Great Western enthusiast – someone recently said that it was a railway you either loved whole heartedly or did not like at all, I think I came somewhere midway between these two extremes – this book would probably be considered incomplete without a view of a modern Great Western engine.

Anyway, here is one of the most famous of all, King George V, seen on arrival at Plymouth North Road on a day excursion with overnight return, from London on 3 April 1931. My wife-to-be, as she was then – we were married in July of the same year – seems to be taking some interest in the engine's inside works, being supervised by a benign representative of the law.

Amongst the many miscellaneous railway subjects I have photographed from time to time are engine nameplates, number plates, makers' works plates, crests and the like. These do not usually make pictures of very wide appeal, being as a rule only of interest to the specialists in such subjects and to model makers.

This photograph is however of particular interest in depicting a *GWR* curved nameplate of standard design, in use for over half a century, and surely the most handsome ever to be designed for the purpose. The general design of the letters – so ornate and attractive compared with the plainer styles usually favoured nowadays, remained standard Swindon practice throughout the rest of the company's existence, and even made its appearance after nationalisation on the diesel 'Warship' class. The somewhat slim form of lettering as depicted here later gave way to a somewhat thicker style, but still of the same general pattern.

The very handsome numerals of *GWR* brass number plates was also a remarkably distinctive design which remained almost unchanged for the best part of a century. The last ones, on 0-6-0PT No 3409, were cast as recently as 1956, and one of these now occupies pride of place in my small collection of such relics.

Engine No 104 *Alliance* was of course one of the three de Glen compound atlantics obtained from France in 1903/5, the works plate being also clearly depicted together with *GWR* crest. It is also a good close-up of the Walschaert's valve gear. Photographed at Oxford on 9 April 1927.

The largest of several independent railways absorbed by the Great Western at the grouping – from a mileage point of view at any rate, was the Cambrian, serving the northern half of the coast of Cardigan Bay from the island points of Oswestry and Whitchurch, with a long branch running southwards to Brecon.

Its passenger traffic was very largely in the hands of a fleet of 4-4-0s of varying age and class, but nearly all of the same general pattern, of which No 1082, shown in this view taken at Oswestry on 28 August 1926, is a good example. This particular engine, late Cambrian No 19, had been built in 1901, and at this time had not yet undergone much Great Westernisation, only the safety valve cover betraying signs of its new ownership, and it had not even acquired a Swindon chimney, so quickly applied to most of the engines.

One of the smaller railways absorbed by the Great Western was the Midland & South Western Junction, an aptly named cross country line running between Cheltenham on the Midland and Andover on the *LSWR*.

Amongst its small but varied locomotive stock were three 2-4-0s, Nos 10-12, which became *GWR* 1334-1336. One of them is seen here in the old roundhouse shed at Reading on 23 August 1930. In the distance can be seen an 'Aberdare' double framed 2-6-0.

These engines lasted a great deal longer than any others from the *M&SWJR*, in fact until the early 1950s. They were also the last of their wheel arrangement to remain at work in this country, and were only outlived by one or two in Ireland, which were still to be found as late as 1961 (see page 53).

The Brill branch was an odd appendage to the Metropolitan system, as completely rural in character as could be found anywhere in the country, and in absolute contrast to the busy Inner Circle line in London which was of course, together with the surburban service out to Aylesbury, the main function of that enterprising railway, absorbed into the London Passenger Transport Board in 1933. The branch was closed in 1935, and traces of most of its former route are now very difficult to identify.

The train is seen here approaching Wood Siding on 22 June 1935, the engine, Beyer Peacock 4-4-0T No 23 then carrying the inscription London Transport on its side tanks, although this cannot be seen in the picture. It is now preserved, being at the time of writing on view in Clapham Museum, but due to be moved elsewhere.

I must apologise for the fact that this is a fairly well known photograph which has appeared several times elsewhere, once in a coloured version, but it seems to merit inclusion in this book.

Aylesbury station, 2 May 1936. An up express to Marylebone standing in the main platform, headed by one of Robinson's handsome atlantics. The chimney is not of the original design, but was at any rate an improvement on the hideous flowerpot type which appeared on so many *GCR* engines after the grouping, completely ruining their appearance. In the bay is a Metropolitan train for Baker Street with one of the 4-4-4Ts, No 104.

The ownership of Aylesbury station was a curious one. Built in 1863, it was purely originally *GWR*, but used also by the Metropolitan after 1892. When the Great Central southern extension to London was built at the end of the century it was in conjunction with the Metropolitan south of Quainton Road. The subsequent formation of the Met & Great Central and the *GWR* and *GCR* Joint Committees in 1906/7 lead to the odd position whereby Aylesbury station and its approaches became the joint property of both of the two joint lines, of which the Great Central was common to both. A joint joint station, in fact, and until quite recently a cast iron notice board bearing the names of both concerns was still to be seen.

During the period just after World War II, from the late 1940s to the early years of nationalisation, when standards of maintenance and cleanliness were at a very low ebb on most railways (and from which many of them never did recover), Kittybrewster, the principal shed of the old Great North of Scotland Railway, was an outstanding exception. Here it was found possible to maintain prewar standards of spick and span smartness, and all of its engines were a joy to behold.

This picture, taken on 16 October 1947, shows one of the four engines used for shunting around Aberdeen docks, No 8191 (recently renumbered from 6844). Note that it still carries the abbreviated initials *NE*, used by the *LNER* during the war years.

A never forgotten excursion, undertaken not from a railway point of view, but in the interests of astronomy.

A total eclipse of the sun took place on 29 June 1927, the only such awe inspiring spectacle visible in Britain for the best part of a century (the next one will not be until 1999) and then only within a narrow belt of country extending mainly through the counties of Lancashire and Yorkshire.

The *LNER* organised a special overnight train from London to Leyburn, one of the suitable spots for witnessing this marvellous spectacle.

This view shows one of the return excursions headed by R class (*LNER* D20) 4-4-0 No 711 piloting S3 class (*LNER* B16) 4-6-0 No 1372. My own train was taken by two S2 (*LNER* B15) 4-6-0s Nos 798 and 819, which worked the train back to Leeds, then taken over by 0-6-0 3535 and 2-6-0 4690 to Doncaster, and atlantic 4442 back to Kings Cross.

A memory of the first privately organised rail tour, run by the Railway Correspondence & Travel Society.

The famous Stirling single No 1 was rooted out by the *LNER* from its hibernation in York Museum, and together with a train of vintage six wheelers it made several trips between Kings Cross and Peterborough or Cambridge, the first ever venture of its kind. These were publicly advertised excursions, but on this particular occasion it was restricted to members of the RCTS and friends, this view being taken at Peterborough on 11 September 1938.

It was not until after the war that it was found possible again to explore the possibilities of this kind of trip, which of course attained an undreamed-of magnitude during the 1950s and 1960s.

An early post war rail tour, again run by the RCTS, 14 April 1951, over a number of lines in East London, including some sections and curves not normally traversed by passenger trains, or over which such services had long since disappeared.

The engine, by special request, was the Great Eastern 0-6-0T usually to be found on pilot duty at Liverpool Street, and always maintained in immaculate condition. Here it had only recently been repainted 'British Railways', in *LNER* apple green, and with its temporary number E8619, later altered to 68619.

A fine view of Durham viaduct, over which a coal train trundles behind North Eastern J25 class 0-6-0 No 1714, built in 1892 and scrapped in 1937. This photograph was taken on 13 May 1936.

It will be noted that, rather unusually, the train is composed entirely of *LNER* wagons, freight trains of this period could usually be relied on to provide a miscellaneous variety of ownerships, both railway and privately owned.

The centre span of the Tay Bridge, with a local southbound train on 3 October 1946, headed by North British 'Scott' class 4-4-0 No 2439 (just lately renumbered from 9498) *Father Ambrose,* built in 1920. It became BR 62439 and was scrapped in 1959.

This was of course the second bridge over the Tay, opened in 1887, and built to replace the earlier one of Thomas Bouch which collapsed in a gale on 28 December 1879 whilst a train was crossing with an estimated loss of eighty lives, there being no survivors.

One of the most difficult photographs I ever obtained, and this only after several attempts at various times. The locality so intrigued me that I always visited it at least once every time I went to Glasgow. The old Caledonian low level line completely in tunnel through the centre of the city was reminiscent of what the Metropolitan Inner Circle must have been like in steam days, perhaps even more so, for the engines using it did not in recent times even have condensing apparatus. Glasgow Central, one of the stations en route, was indeed an eerie place, with an almost unnatural quietness broken every minute or so by the rumble of the trams which could be heard passing overhead. In the tunnels in particular, the fumes could be almost overpowering, yet nostalgically at least a delight to the connoisseur, one would give a good deal to savour such an aroma once more. What a pity some of this good honest coal smoke could not have been bottled in some way for the enjoyment, or at least education, of the present-day enthusiast, brought up with the smell of diesel fumes in their nostrils. I know which I should prefer!

This picture, taken on 19 September 1955, shows Stanier 2-6-2T No 40187 on a through train from Rutherglen to Dumbarton. It was necessarily a time exposure, and shows the wreaths of steam plus smoke circling overhead.

The *NBR* had a somewhat similar underground line through the city, but this was rather more of the 'cut and cover' method of construction and not nearly so smokey. Like its *LMS* counterpart at Central it ran beneath the *LNER* station at Queen Street. It is now electrified (the *LMS* route has been entirely closed). This view, taken on 11 August 1930, shows a *GNR* N2 0-6-2T No 4736 at Charing Cross. At first sight, any Londoner unaware of its Glasgow namesake, might be a little startled at seeing this picture which he would at once connect with the much better known centre in the southern metropolis.

Good snow scenes are not very easy to obtain in this country; one requires the rare combination of a good snowfall followed by bright sunshine. Usually it is a dull and overcast sky making such a subject as a moving train difficult to photograph satisfactorily.

Perfect conditions did however apply for a day or two in early March 1947, there had been about two feet of snow, with clear skies predominating in the following days and I was able to take advantage of the conditions to obtain a good many local shots. (We will not go too closely into how it happened that I was at home during that period when I had no leave due to me and nominally I should have been at work in London.)

This picture was obtained at Northchurch cutting on 7 March 1947 and shows pacific No 6220 *Coronation* heading a down express.

It was not often that a Gresley A3 pacific could be seen on a humdrum freight duty, but No 60055 *Woolwinder* is seen here on 31 July 1948 leaving Hadley Wood tunnel.

This was in early BR days, and the engine, although renumbered, still sports *LNER* livery with 'British Railways' on the tender.

It was of course before the very necessary widening of this awkward bottleneck of two lines to four (including the construction of an additional tunnel) was undertaken.

Verney Junction, on the cross country *LNWR* line between Bletchley and Oxford, which unfortunately no longer has a passenger service, greatly missed as it was a most useful east to west link, as was the eastern link to Cambridge, part of which is now entirely closed.

This was one of those stations, situated in the open countryside, remote from any centre of population, the tiny village consisting of an inn, and a few houses could hardly be said to come within this category, and passenger traffic was naturally always very scanty, even though it formed the outer terminus of through Metropolitan trains from London. it was also the junction for the *LNWR* branch to Banbury.

This view, taken on 2 May 1936, shows an Oxford-Cambridge train hauled by Webb 'Cauliflower' 0-6-6 No 8535, built in 1900. It later became No 28535, and lasted until 1947.

The Lancashire & Yorkshire always seemed to get left out in the earlier years when my long excursions were limited both by time and money, and when I was able to travel any distance it was Scotland which was my main objective, usually overnight, and the *L & YR* got bypassed in consequence. It was in any case not a line which attracted me greatly, it had fewer old engines, what there were being much standardised, and with hardly any interesting oddities.

However, on my first visit to Manchester in 1926, I was very pleased to find this jolly little 4-4-0 No 997, still in pregrouping livery at Victoria station, on June 7 of that year.

It is a lasting regret that I missed out on the unique inside cylinder atlantics, 'the highflyers'. I did get one, but it was taken in a hurry, and I made an exposure error, resulting in a very poor picture.

One of the six very fine Glasgow & South Western 4-6-4Ts built by Whitelegg in 1922, chiefly for the fast services to Ayr and similar places on the system.

Photographed at St Enoch, Glasgow, on 11 April 1930. Another of the class can be seen in the distance, together with a much earlier engine, 4-4-0 No 14135, built at Kilmarnock in 1885.

The 4-6-4Ts, Nos 15400-15405, former *G&SWR*, Nos 540-545, were all withdrawn during 1935 and 1936.

The well known Caledonian single wheeler, was almost (but not quite, see page 43) the last single wheeler to remain in regular service in the British Isles. It was however certainly the final 4-2-2 express engine, outlasting the Midland Johnson singles by several years.

Built by Neilson & Co in 1886 for the Edinburgh exhibition, after which it was taken over by the *CR*, it was the only one of its class, and took part in the 1888 Race to Scotland. For a number of years after World War I it was used for hauling the directors' saloon, but in the early 1930s was put to ordinary passenger work on the easy line between Perth and Dundee.

Seen here near Magdalen Green on 19 May 1930, then still in *LMS* red, but it was subsequently repainted black. Withdrawn in 1935 and restored to *CR* blue for preservation. Put into working order in 1957 and worked on rail tours all over the country for several years. Now in Glasgow Museum.

Scene on the Cromford & High Peak Railway, 4 May 1934. This somewhat out of the way goods line over the moorland of the Derbyshire Peak District attained a maximum height at one point of 1265 feet above sea level reached by three inclines, two of them cable worked, operated by beam engines; the third, depicted here, by ordinary adhesion. This picture was taken at the point where the gradient steepens near the summit, from 1 in 20 to the maximum of 1 in 14, the most severe in the country so worked. This was only just possible by taking a run at the incline, an initial sixty mph sometimes being attained until a derailment in 1937 resulted in a limit of forty mph being imposed, with a reduction in load to four wagons. If the engine failed to make the summit it had to return to the starting point for a second charge.

This view shows such a train going all out near the top, with a North London 0-6-0T No 7527, several of which were drafted to the line at this period. The engines must have found the moorland air a sharp contrast to the smokey and grimy atmosphere of north east London to which they had been previously accustomed.

Photography during the war was difficult, as one was viewed with great suspicion, and on one or two occasions at Derby (to which town my firm had been evacuated, quite fortuitously, but it could hardly have been a better choice from my point of view) during 1940 and 1941, I narrowly escaped arrest! I had more or less to give up the attempt, losing many maddeningly interesting scenes as a consequence.

In 1942 His Majesty duly notified me that he required my services, and I spent two not very happy years with the RAOC. Anyway, we were able to take a conventional seaside holiday in 1941, the only one I ever had since about 1911, when I remember the sea front somewhere between Westcliff and Leigh on Sea, when even then I was more interested in the green *LT&SR* engines in the background than digging sand castles on the shore. This time, at Llanfairfechan on the North Wales coast line I managed to find an hotel overlooked by the railway. To secure a back bedroom facing it was easy, as more normal people preferred a front sea view. From here I was able to get a number of pictures. This one, taken on 19 July 1941 shows a Llandudno Junction-Bangor local hauled by *LNWR* 'Precursor' No 25277 Oberon.

A couple of examples of my very small collection of foreign subjects, taken on the only two occasions I have ever crossed the English Channel. The first of these was a four day trip organised by the Stephenson Locomotive Society over Easter 1930, when we toured the railways of Holland. A marvellous collection of engines we found, too, ranging from modern 4-6-0s down to many old 2-4-0s and 4-4-0s, many of them English built by Beyer Peacock, with those fine distinctive features. Of special interest were five atlantics, a type which has always been extremely popular with enthusiasts, but these were distinctly unusual in that they had inside cylinders. Apart from the famous *L&YR* 'high flyers', and one solitary example on the *GNR*, atlantics seem to have been almost invariably outside cylindered. These Dutch engines, however, were all the more unusual in having outside frames, being possibly unique in this respect. It is believed that the last atlantics to remain in service anywhere in the world are four still to be found at work in Mozambique in 1971.

This photograph was taken at Eindhoven on 20 April 1930.

My second venture beyond the shores of Great Britain and Ireland was a day trip run by the Railway Correspondence and Travel Society on 4 July 1937, outwards via Folkestone and Calais, back via Boulogne.

Still on the atlantic theme, I was fortunate in finding some of the former 'de Glens' still in service, these were of course the forerunners of the well known pacifics, which were so much sought after during the last decade of steam on the boat trains between Calais and Paris.

This atlantic, Nord No 2-663, was photographed at Calais.

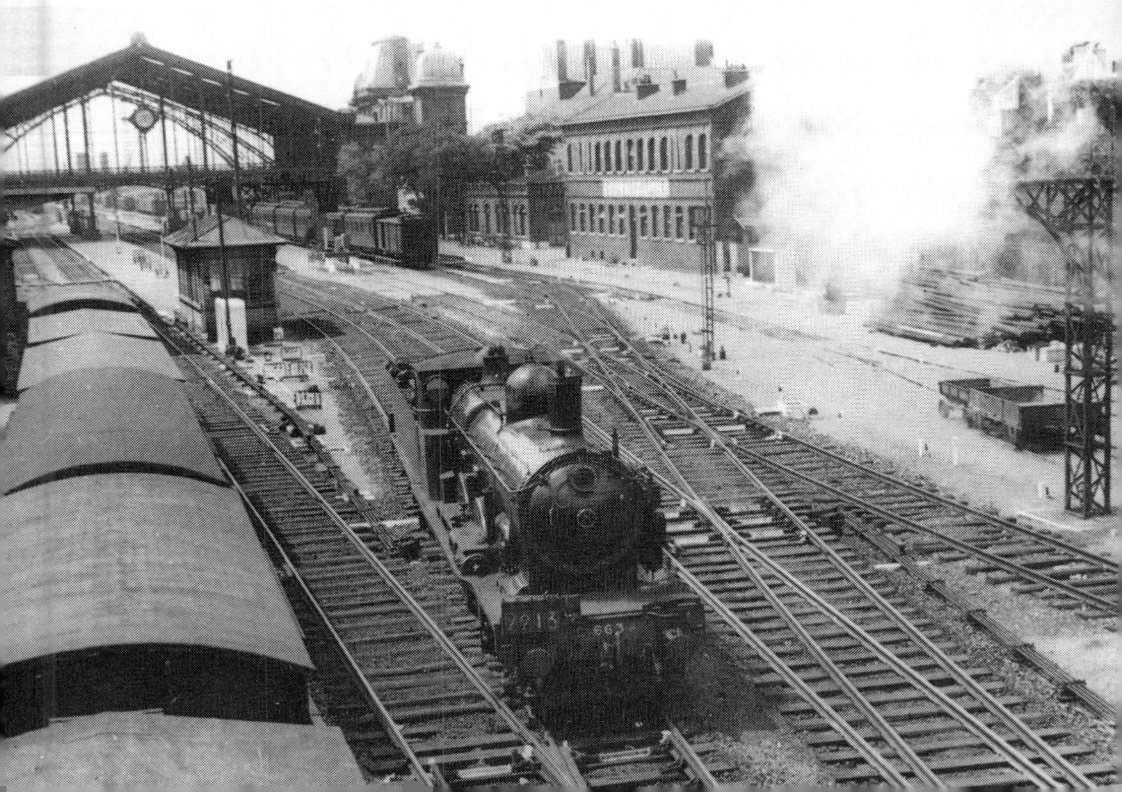

To finish with just one 'off beat' unusual shot. It could sometimes happen under certain conditions, when travelling by train, that one could see the shadow of the engine on the side of a cutting, given that the sun was low in the sky and that one was travelling near to the front, the leading coach for the best effect. I made several attempts to photograph this spectacle at odd occasions over the years, of which this is probably the most effective.

No prizes are offered for identifying the type of locomotive which was in fact a London and North Western 2-4-2T, and for what the information is worth, it was No 6628, taken somewhere near Widnes, on 26 April 1951.

THEMES

It is the publisher's request that in the interests of uniformity the picture selections in this series of books should comprise three main definite themes, with a fourth section consisting of subjects not within any of these categories.

My first choice is 'The Midland and the Highland'. A rather odd combination perhaps, but nevertheless my two favourite railways, the *MR* from very earliest days, and the Highland, with which I fell in love on my first visit in 1927. The two lines had little in common except the lovely crimson lake colour, which at that time applied to all passenger engines on the *HR*, as to the other constituents of the *LMS*, in Scotland and to a lesser extent on the *LNWR* and *L&YR*. Whatever the field of one's special interests in this life, I suppose one always has a main favourite outstanding above all others. Just as in music – my second great interest – where Wagner stands firmly much above the many other contenders, so the Midland has remained consistently my first choice. It is remarkable how many railway enthusiasts have these two such widely varying spheres of interest in common, far greater than mere coincidence could provide. It may be a more than usual ability to appreciate some of the more beautiful aspects of life, for there is no doubt that the steam locomotive can rank among one of man's most lovely creations.

For my second theme I chose, after some deliberation, 'Light and Independent Railways', as I have always found them, together with branch lines, of very high priority in my field of interest.

Thirdly, the railways of Ireland, which I first discovered in 1929, and which between the wars were an enthusiast's sheer delight. One could re-live the atmosphere of the railways of England – with which they had much in common, but at about the period of thirty years or so earlier. I was able to enjoy about a dozen wonderful trips to this haven of nostalgia, interrupted only by the war, until it succumbed to the inevitable diesel age.

Where else, for instance, would it have been possible as late as 1955 to travel, as my son and I did, on an express mail train on a 134 mile main line journey behind a vintage 2-4-0, and the miscellaneous make-up of the train including an Edwardian twelve-wheeled clerestory dining car, gaslit?

In a book of this sort there must inevitably be a certain proportion of one's most outstanding efforts which have already appeared elsewhere, but in many cases not for many years, in publications no longer obtainable, and which will perhaps be new to some of the younger generation. There are also some never previously published pictures which I hope will be of interest.

My first camera was a model No 2 folding 'Brownie' 3½ x 2½in, with f/8 Rapid Rectilinear lens with focusing adjustment, giving good definition for that class of camera, really only intended for the 'happy snaps at the seaside' kind of photography. For more serious work, especially during the winter months when I first started, it was necessary to use a tripod giving exposures of a half-second or more on the comparatively slow emulsion speeds then available. Moving subjects were impracticable, even in bright sunshine, with maximum shutter speeds of only 1/25 or 1/50 second.

After about eighteen months of reasonably satisfactory results within these severe limitations it was obviously necessary to get something more ambitious if I was to take up the hobby seriously. My choice fell on a Butcher 'Popular Pressman' ¼ plate reflex, using glass plates, which I found more satisfactory for critical work than the films of the period. This gave yeoman service for some sixteen years, then in 1937 I changed over to the then up-and-coming 35mm miniature film, and obtained a Leica with f3.5 lens. Even at that time it cost about £100, a lot of money in those days, but it proved a sound investment, and after getting used to a somewhat different technique it stood me in good stead for many years. Unfortunately it was stolen in 1963, but I was so satisfied and used to its performance that I replaced it with an identical model which I still use.

I am sometimes asked how many photographs I have taken over the span of fifty odd years. This is not too easy to calculate, as although all of my negatives are catalogued and indexed this includes quite a lot of non-railway subjects, and the numbering scheme for various reasons does not run consecutively. This again sometimes raises a query, so perhaps I could briefly explain that, starting with photograph No 1 on 14 December 1919, already referred to in the introduction, the list ran continuously to 14999 in early 1937, when with the Leica I started a new series at 40000. However, when my son took in turn his first photograph in 1944, I decided that looking ahead on a long term basis, in the hope that he would follow in my footsteps, as in fact he has done, it would be better to integrate from the start to avoid future confusion. He therefore began at 70000 (shades of 'Britannia', then yet undreamed of, and still to come – and go!), and, by the time he reached 71999 I had already gone forward from 72000. He therefore took up the running at 82000, continuing to 86999, after which he reverted to the big gap starting at 17000, whilst I went on from 87000 and now run into six figures.

Whereas my annual taking at the highest peak, from about 1947 to 1959 was in the region of over 2000, it has now dropped to about 200 per year, with so little of interest left to take anyway, and it is perhaps just as well in view of advancing years.

In all, however, I estimate about 60000 railway subjects of all sorts (of my own taking) in some fifty-two years.